Prussian Nights

Alexander Solzhenitsyn

PRUSSIAN NIGHTS

A POEM

TRANSLATED BY ROBERT CONQUEST

Farrar, Straus and Giroux · NEW YORK

Russian text first published by YMCA-Press, Paris, under the title
Прусские Ночи
Copyright © 1974 by A. Soljenitsyne
Translation copyright © 1977 by Robert Conquest
All rights reserved
Published simultaneously in Canada
by McGraw-Hill Ryerson Ltd., Toronto
Printed in the United States of America
DESIGNED BY HERB JOHNSON

FIRST EDITION, 1977

Library of Congress Cataloging in Publication Data

Solzhenitsyn, Aleksandr Isaevich
Prussian nights : a poem
Translation of Prusskie nochi
1. World War, 1939-1945—Poetry.   I. Title.
PG3488.04P813   1977   891.7′1′44   77-3298

CONTENTS

Prussian Nights

Прусские Ночи

Расступись, земля чужая!
Растворяй свои ворота!
Это наша удалая
Едет русская пехота!
Холмик, падь, мосток и холмик –
Стой! Сходи! По карте – тут.
Будет злая ведьма помнить
В небе зимнем наш салют!
Столько лет всё ближе, ближе
Подбирались, шли, ползли –
«Бат-тарея! Слушай! Трижды
В небо прусское – пали!!»
Шестьдесят их в ветрожоге
Смуглых, зло-веселых лиц.
По машинам! По дороге!
На Европу! – навались!
Враг – ни запахом, ни слухом.
Распушили пухом-духом!
Эх, закатим да-ле-ко!..
Только что-то нам дико
И на сердце не легко.
Странно глянуть сыздаля,
А вблизи – того дивней:
Непонятная земля,
Всё не так, как у людей,
Не как в Польше, не как дома –
Крыши кроют не соломой,

OPEN up, you alien country!
Wide open let your gates be thrown!
For, approaching, see how boldly
Russia's battle line rolls on!
Hillock, dip, small bridge, and hillock—
Halt! Check on the map— We're there.
Dismount! The foul witch* shall remember
Our salvo on the wintry air!
How many years now we've been stalking,
Walking nearer, crawling near . . .
"Bat-tery! Into the sky of Prussia—
Load!— Ready! Three rounds!— Fire!"
There were wickedly cheerful faces,
Sixty of them, wind-burned, black.
Into your vehicles! Get moving!
Into Europe now!— Attack!
Of the enemy no whiff or whisper.
Ah, we've thrashed him good and proper!
We'll roll on far . . . far . . . But what starts
Up in us? Some strangeness hurts.
There's no lightness in our hearts.
Odd enough, seen from a distance,
It's quite astounding from up close:
A land beyond our understanding,
Nothing's like what it is with us!
It's not like Poland is, or home is—
Their roofs aren't thatched, their barns are firm as

*Witch: Germany. (A.S.)

И сараи – под хоромы.
Как обрезало по мете –
Вьется путь по незнакомой,
По незнаемой планете.
Не по нашей русской мерке
Отработаны, шалишь,
Крутоскатных островерхих
Колпаки высоких крыш.
А и нам бы так годится,
Зря ругнули сгоряча:
Черепица, черепица,
Башни, теремы да шпицы
Да дома из кирпича.
Эт' и нам бы не плачевно,
Эт' и нам бы по душе –
Что саша́ – через деревню,
Что деревня – на саше́.
Темным клубом из-за леса
Низко тучи наплывают.
Зимних сумерок завеса
Мглою к сердцу подступает.
Ночь долга, а день недолог.
Что дрожит там в гуще ёлок?
Нет ли немцев? Что-то чудно..
Что-то слишком уж безлюдно.
Там вон, в хвое – вроде двое?..
Чтоб душа была в покое –
Поджигай дома, братва!!

Mansions cut from solid timbers.
As though with square and line they'd done it,
The road rolls on through an unknown,
An unknowable new planet.
It wasn't in the Russian fashion
—You bet!—that they finished off
The gables on the steeply sided,
High sharp ridges of the roof.
We could do with things like theirs,
Not have mocked them quite so quick:
Tiles, tiles—and see the towers,
All the turrets and the spires,
And houses built of solid brick.
We'd not be sorry to have suchlike!
Things like that are pretty good!
A highway runs through every village:
Each village—on a real road!
Floating from behind the forest
Low cloud's appearing, massy, dark.
The veil of the winter twilight
Rises hazy on the heart.
Long nights now. Short days. But hush! Is
Something rustling in the bushes?
Germans? . . . We've seen too few people . . .
It's strange . . . Down there among the trees
Where the pine needles heap—a couple?
Just to set our minds at ease
—Burn the houses down, my brothers!

Эх, займется живо-мило!
Да не снизу! – под стропила! –
Под стропила, голова!..
Пусто ль ехать нам, ребятки,
Немцу память не оставив?! –
Без команды, в беспорядке
Там и сям, гляди, – десятки
Дымно-красных мутных зарев!
Ну ж и крепко, ну ж и ловко
Отомщаем мы врагу! –
Всё в огне! ищи ночевку!
Видно, спать нам на снегу.
Ладно! Нам выходит туго,
Ну, и ехали ж не зря:
Расцветает над округой
Небывалая заря!
И несется наша лава
С гиком, свистом, блеском фар –
Кляйн Козлау, Гросс Козлау –
Что деревня – то пожар!
Всё в огне!! Мычат коровы,
Заперты в горящих хлевах, –
　　　　Эх, милаши,
　　　　　Вы не наши!
Нам самим бы по-здорову...
И направо, и налево
Вьются, рвутся, пляшут змеи!
С двух сторон взнеслось столбами,

Ah, look how it's taking hold!
The walls won't catch?— Well, start the rafters!
Fire the rafters first, you dolt!
No point in driving on—eh, fellows?—
Unless we leave them some mementos?
Without orders, as it takes us,
Here, there, everywhere, look—scores
Of smoky-red, dark-gleaming fires!
Well, now we're getting our revenge, lads,
We've hit him good and hard, the foe!
Everything's aflame. —Nightquarters?
We'll have to spend it in the snow.
Oh, well, that's bad! But all the same,
We've given *them* a tougher time:
The whole district sees a dawn
The like of which it's never known!
Our columns pour ahead like lava
With wild cries, whistling, headlights' glare
—Klein Koslau, Gross Koslau—
Every village—is now a fire!
Everything flames. Locked in their burning
Cowsheds, how the cows are bellowing—
          Ah, poor creatures
          But you're not ours!
What's more, we have ourselves to save . . .
For right and left, on either side,
What serpents rush and dance and glide!
On either side what columns rise,

С двух сторон сплелось над нами,
Пылью огненной, звездами,
Искрой, блёсткой, головнями
Так и сыпет нам на шею.
Ветер огненный по школе
В книгах рыскает, голодный.
Самодельно крыты толем
Шесть машин моих походных.
Нам самим бы не сгореть тут!
На подножку. Смех и грех.
И кричу в румяном свете:
«По махальщику – наверх!»
Взобрались. Полой шинели
Машут, пашут, отметают.
Ну, спасибо, пролетели!
Ухо-парни, службу знают!

Площадь. Сгрудились машины.
Жили, дьяволы, богато!
Вот когда вы, ИМЕНИНЫ
НЕИЗВЕСТНОГО СОЛДАТА!
Шнапс хлобыщут из бутылки,
Тащат смокинги в посылки –
Что ты будешь с солдатнёй?
Кто-то скачет на кобылке,
Крестит небо головнёй.
Разбрелись, пируют, шарят.
В лица пышет, в лица жарит.

On either side roofs meet the skies
—Made of fiery dust, of stars,
Of embers, glimmerings, and sparks
Which shower down on our bended necks.
In the school the fiery wind
Hunts hungrily among the books.
And there's only rough tarpaulin
We made ourselves, on my six trucks.
Better watch *we* don't catch fire!
On the running board. It's funny and grim.
I shout into the rosy glare,
"One on each roof to sweep it clear!"
Up they clamber. With their greatcoats'
Skirts they flap and sweep and shove
The sparks aside. —Ah, now we're through it.
Smart lads! They really know their stuff!

A square. It's chockablock with cars.
The devils! You can see that they
Certainly lived well. But now,
Now it's Unknown Soldier Day!
Some swig schnapps from the bottle. Some
Grab dinner jackets to send home.
What can you do with the soldiery?
One, riding around on an old nag,
Waves to the sky with a charred log.
They're scattered about, to feast and loot.
Their faces shine and burn in the heat.

В золотом огне сгорев,
Провалилась крыша в хлев.
Из-под новых темных кровель
Валом валит черный дым –
Завоёванного кровью
Никому не отдадим!
Кто-то, руки в растопырку,
Загонявшись, ловит кур, –
И над всем возносит кирха
Свой готический ажур.
Д' ну ж и жарко, д' ну ж и ярко,
       Как при солнце,
         Будто днем!
Как бы кирху нам под арку,
Вон, под верхнее оконце,
Подцепить бы язычком?!
Пир и власть! Ликует хаос!
Ничего душе не жаль!
Кто-то выбил дверь в Gasthaus
И оттуда прет – рояль!!
В дверь не лезет – и с восторгом
Бьет лопатой по струнам:
«Ах ты, утварь! Значит, нам,
Не достанешься, бойцам?
Не оставлю Военторгу,
Интендантам и штабам!»

Consumed there in the golden fire,
A roof's collapsed into a byre.
From under dark and new-built eaves now
Black smoke's billowing in a flood.
We won't let others lay their hands on
What we won with our own blood!
Someone's trying to catch a hen there
With open arms, exhaustedly.
Above it all the chapel rises
With its Gothic tracery.
It's sure hot. It's sure bright too.
    Like sunshine,
    It might be day!
How about starting up a new
Fire in the church, under that fine
Arch up by the window bay?
Feasting and power! Exultant chaos!
There's nothing we'll have regrets about.
Someone breaks into the Gasthaus
And pushes a grand piano out!
Unable to drag it through the door,
He bangs the strings with an old spade
And utters a delighted roar,
"If you can't be had by the warrior,
Staff and Supply won't get you either,
You swine—or Military Trade!"*

*Military Trade (Voentorg) : organization in charge of sales of consumer
goods to the military. At this time it often used war booty as stock.

Кто-то бродит беззаботно,
Знатно хряпнул, развезло, –
И со звоном палкой вотмашь
Бьет оконное стекло:
«Где прошел я – там не буду!
Бей хрусталь, дроби посуду,
Вспоминайте молодца!
Добро ль, худо ль, янки-дудль,
Лам-ца-дрица! лам-ца-ца!»
Рвет и рвет, как склад патронов,
Черепицу сгоряча.
Вдоль деревни запаленной,
Красным светом озаренный,
Сыпет Ванька ублаженный
И – в гармонику сплеча:
«Ра-азменяйте мне сорок миллионов
И купите билет до Сергача!!»
Знай лады перебирает,
И коровы умирают,
Обезумевши мыча.
«Заплатил братан мой смертью,
Заплатить бы мог и я...»
«По машинам! Что вы, черти!
Впереди добра, друзья!!..»
И – к пожару от пожара,
Снег под скатами буря,
И выхватывают фары,
Мертвым светом серебря,

Another lurches without a care,
Far gone in booze, it's pretty plain,
Taking a resounding bash
At the nearest windowpane.
"Once I've gone I won't be back.
China—shatter! Crystal—crack!
And you'll remember this fine lad!
Yankee-Doodle to good and bad!
Rumty-tumty-clickety-clack!"
Like a stack of burning shells,
The roof throws off exploding tiles.
Triumphant through the blazing village,
Lit up by the red flames' brilliance,
Vanka's strutting, half off balance,
And on his squeeze-box plays a catch,
"G-i-ive me change for forty millions
And buy me a ticket to Sergach!"*
He runs his fingers up the keys.
Mad bellows come from dying cows.
"He paid—yes, with his life—my comrade.
I too might have paid with mine . . ."
"Into your trucks! Come on, you devils!
The loot ahead is extra fine!"
So on we go, from fire to fire,
Our tires are churning up the snow.
And, silver-plating all before us
With a dead shine, the headlights glow

*A small town in Gorki Province.

Нескончаемую просадь
Буков, липок и дубков,
Гильзы, ящики набросом
И обломки передков.
Снова зарево растет.
Локоть, мостик, поворот –
Всё в огне! Но чудеса:
Заводские корпуса
Пощадили небеса
И столпившийся народ
У распахнутых ворот.
Мне стучит в стекло кабины
Лейтенант неутомимый:
«Разрешите выслать взвод
На разведку в спиртзавод?
Десять новеньких канистров
У меня, вишь, завалялись..»
«Но – ни капли в рот! И быстро!»
«Для науки! На анализ!»
«Знаешь, там этил, метил...»
Но уже он соскочил.
Взявши в руки большемерный
С долгим череном черпак,
Ловко взлазит на цистерну
Старый бес, седой казак.
Помахал толпе папахой,
Окрестился вольным взмахом:
«Помолитесь, христиане!
Умираю – ради вас!»
Зачерпнул, понюхал, глянул –
Опрокинул, будто квас.

On endless lines of roadside-planted
Beeches, limes, and little oaks,
Cartridge cases, cartridge boxes,
Limbers with axles smashed, and spokes.
The glow grows brighter once again.
Sharp curve; small bridge; turn, and then
—What flames! But, for a wonder, see
Heaven has spared that factory,
And a rough crowd congregates
Around its widely open gates.
An indefatigable subaltern
Knocks upon my cabin's pane,
"May I take a troop out? We
Should reconnoiter that distillery!
It just so happens, by some chance,
I've ten large unused empty cans."
"But not a drop to drink! Be quick!"
"For science. For analysis."
"It contains ethyl, methyl . . . yes . . ."
But he's already jumped down back.
An old devil, a gray Cossack
Leaped lightly up onto the vat.
He grabbed a huge, long-handled scoop.
He waved his shaggy sheepskin hat,
Making a broad Sign of the Cross.
With "Christians, pray! For you I die!"
He scooped it, sniffed it, gave a sly
Glance, and tossed it off like kvass.

Крякнул, вытер сивый ус:
    «Ух, чертяка!
    И спиртяка!
Навалитесь, добры люди!
    Хоть за вкус
    Не берусь,
Горяченько будет!!»
Не дослушав, повалили:
Ай, спасибо казаку!
Коммиссары – разрешили!!
Трибуналы – в отпуску!!

Снова катим, снова катим
По пылающей земле,
И мотив из Сарасатэ
Так и вьется в уши мне –
Неотстанный, непоборный,
Зов лукавый, не военный;
    «Этот веер черный!
    Веер драгоценный!»
Величаво и зловеще
Труд пылает вековой.
Пламя плещет, пламя хлещет
У меня над головой.
То багрово, жирно, жадно
Языком махнет в окно,

He grunted, wiped his gray mustache.
      "Devils in Hell!
       What alcohol!
     Good people, come along!
       I wouldn't boast
        About the taste,
      But I guarantee it's strong!"
They rush! Our thanks, you old Cossack,
For what we here receive!
The commissars—have said O.K.!
Courts-martial—gone on leave!

Again on the move, again on the move,
Across the ever-smoldering ground.
In my ears a Sarasate*
Theme is going round and round.
It won't be quiet, it won't die,
Unmilitary, a cunning cry:
        "Here's a fan, a black one!
         It's a very precious fan!"
Majestic, ominous round me now
To flame the work of centuries turns,
Fire is weaving, fire is lashing,
Above my head it burns and burns.
Crimson it grows, and fat and greedy,
Its tongue from a window now it thrusts

*Pablo Martín Melintón Sarasate y Narascuez, 1844–1908, violinist and
composer of sensuous music, popular in Russia.

То над башенкой оно
Располощется нарядно,
Златоструйно, многоскладно,
Огневое полотно.
И опять он, и опять он,
Из-за черно-красных пятен,
Зол, торжественен, понятен,
Соблазнительно игрив,
Тот же дьявольский мотив,
Тем же крадущимся скерцо,
Всё сильнее, всё сильнее:
   «Ну, какое сердце
   Устоять сумеет?!..»

Что ж, гори, дыми, пылай,
Трудолюбный гордый край.
Средь неистовства толпы
Мести в сердце не ношу.
Не сожгу в тебе щепы.
И дворца не погашу.
Я пройду, тебя не тронув,
Как Пилат омыв персты.
Меж тобой и мной – Самсонов,
Меж тобой и мной – кресты
Русских косточек белеют.
Чувства странные владеют
В эту ночь моей душой:

Above a little tower unrolled,
Charmingly, in threads of gold,
A tapestry with many a fold,
A fire cloth fluttering in the gusts.
And again now, and again now,
From behind the red-black patches,
Irresistible, portentous, evil,
Temptingly, work of a devil,
Music of that same theme catches
—Hear the same slinking scherzo start.
Stronger it grows, stronger it grows:
      "And oh, what heart
        Could well oppose?"

Well, land industrious and proud,
Blaze and smoke and flame away.
Amid the violence of the crowd,
In my heart no vengeance calls.
I'll not fire one stick of kindling,
Yet I'll not quench your flaming halls.
Untouched I'll leave you. I'll be off
Like Pilate when he washed his hands.
Between us, there is Samsonov,*
Between us many a cross there stands
Of whitened Russian bones. For strange
Feelings rule my soul tonight.

*General A. V. Samsonov, 1859–1914, commanded the Russian Second Army
in the disastrous 1914 campaign.

Ты давно мне не чужой.
Нас сплело с тобой издавна
Своевольно, своенравно.
Шли в Берлин прямой чертой,
Я с надеждой, с беспокойством
Озирался – не свернуть бы.
Я предчувствовал, Ostpreußen,
Что скрестятся наши судьбы!
Там, у нас, погребено
Пылью лет, архивов тайной
То, что вами взнесено
Спесью башен в Хохенштайне,
Что́ забыть мне не дано,
Знать и помнить велено:
Как четырнадцатым годом
Вот по этим же проходам,
Межозерным дефиле,
Вот по этой же земле,
В шесть солдатских переходов
От снабженья, от тылов, –
За Париж, за чудо Марны
Гнали слепо и бездарно
Сгусток русских корпусов.
Без разведки и без хлеба
Гнали в ноги Людендорфу,
А потом под синим небом
Их топили в черном торфе.

I've known you now for all these years.
Yet, long ago, mere chance it was,
Mere caprice, that bound us tight.
Already, marching on Berlin,
Both anxious then and hopeful, I'd
Look around—for fear we'd turn aside.
Long since, a premonition rose,
Ostpreussen! that our paths would cross.
Back home, beneath the dust of years
Secret archives hold unseen
What your arrogance thrust up
In the towers of Hohenstein.
I'm bound in duty to recall
How in '14, on this same soil,
By the same road our army takes,
This defile here between the lakes
—For Paris, the Miracle of the Marne—*
With bungling brain and blinder eyes
They drove them down, a six-day march
From their supports, from their supplies,
A knot of Russian Army Corps
Without reconnaissance, without bread,
To Ludendorff, beneath his feet;
And then, a blue sky overhead,
They drowned them there in the black peat.

*The Russian invasion was designed to relieve the pressure on France;
and in fact it led to a diversion of German troops, without which the French
might well have failed to win the Battle of the Marne and save Paris.

Шедший выручить, от смыка
Был отозван Нечволодов... –
Затая в себе до крика
Стыд и боль того похода,
В храмном сумраке читален,
Не делясь, юнец, ни с кем,
Я склонялся над листами
Пожелтевших карт и схем,
И кружочки, точки, стрелки
Оживали предо мной
То болотной перестрелкой,
То сумятицей ночной.
Жажда. Голод. Август. Зной.
Дико вскинутые морды
Рвущих упряжь лошадей
И не части – орды, орды
Обезумевших людей...

А теперь несется лава
С гиком, свистом, блеском фар:
Виндткен, Ваплиц и Орлау –
Что деревня – то пожар!
Роют, треплют и ворошат,
Самоходки стены крошат,
В прорву проволок и надолб,

And as he marched to their relief
Nechvolodov* was recalled . . .
I nursed inside me till I filled
With muffled shouting, all the pain,
And all the shame, of that campaign.
In the dark cathedral gloom
Of one or another reading room
I shared with none my boyish grief,
I bent over the yellowed pages
Of those aging maps and plans,
Till little circles, dots, and arrows
Came alive beneath my hands,
Now as a fire fight in the marshes,
Now as a tumult in the night:
Thirst. Hunger. August. Heat.
—Now the wildly lunging muzzles
Of horses tearing at the rein,
Now broken units turned to raving
Mobs of men who'd gone insane . . .

And still our columns pour like lava
With wild cries, whistling, headlights' glare
—Windtchen, Waplitz, and Orlau—
Every village—is now a fire!
The self-propelled artillery then,
Turning, burrowing, heaving, pushing,
Crumbles walls and finds the gaps

*A general in Samsonov's campaign.

Поверх сровненных траншей,
Валит русская громада
Жерл, моторов и людей!
Только-только осветило
Лес и поле серым светом, –
Небо всуплошь кроют ИЛы
К немцу с утренним приветом!
Гулом радостным победы
Полнят душу, дразнят слух:
Пушки-гаубицы едут
С т а п я т и д е с я т и д в у х –
Чтоб поспеть, не спя ночами,
Тракторами-тягачами
Тарахтят без остановки
(Сколько весишь – там не спросят);
Лихо вихрем левой бровкой
Студебекеры проносят
Легкой стайкой трехдюймовки –
«Эй, т р у б а! Конец держи!»;
На т р и ч е т в е р т и Доджи
Мчат и мчат с о р о к а п я т к и,
Те, что с горечью ребятки
«Прощай, родина!» зовут;
Вперебой им, там и тут,
Шатко, валко, вперепрыжку
По раскатанной земле –
Минометы-коротышки

Among the wire and tank traps.
—Made of gun muzzles, engines, men,
The Russian juggernaut is rushing
Over trenches beaten flat!
Dawn has just begun to cast a
Gray light over wood and pasture—
Il-2's through the skies returning
Wish the Germans a Good Morning!
Victory's voice with all its joys
—Heartwarming but ear-splitting noise—
Mounts, with a new lot breaking loose:
Howitzers—they're 152's.
Having rendezvous to keep
Behind their tractor-type transporters,
They don't stop nighttime and don't sleep
(No weight checks here to hold them up.)
Whirling down the left-hand file,
Studebakers, to support us,
Are hauling lighter three-inch cannons:
"Hey, there, stovepipe! Grab our tail!"
Dodges—the three-quarter-ton ones—
Rush the forty-fives to fight
—The ones our bitter lads have christened
With the name of "Goodbye, homeland!"
Mixing with them here and yon,
Shaking, swaying, bumping on,
Over earth the tracks have flattened,
"Shorty" mortars ride in place

За задками Шевроле;
А для самой модной драки,
Кто не видел – посмотри,
Тянут янки-автотраки
Пушки русских БС-три! –
Друг за дружкой, друг за дружкой
Едут новенькие пушки,
Долгоствольны, дальнобойны,
Нет таких еще нигде.
До прорыва бьют спокойно
С огневых, как АДД.
Чуть прорыв – туда их ветром,
На наводочку прямую,
Т и г р у на два километра
Прошибают л о б о в у ю!
Поздний плод большой науки,
Проползают танки-щуки!
Снявши с рельс своих полотна,
Чередой, в притирку, плотно,
Не идут – плывут заботно
С полным грузом спелых мин
Три восьмерки к а т е р и н.
Год назад оравы пешей
Что́ тянулось вдоль шоссе! –
Умудрил теперь их леший,
На машинах вся и все!
Обнаглевшая пехота

At the back of Chevrolets.
But for fashionable battles—
You've not seen them? Take a glance:
—At those Yankee half-tracks pulling
Russian BS-3-type guns.
There they roll, mile after mile,
Cannon in the latest style!
Long-range, long-barreled, you'd not seek
Them elsewhere. No, they're quite unique!
Behind the front they fire serenely,
As their heavy brother fights.
A breakthrough calls—they're there like lightning,
Firing over open sights,
And, still two thousand meters from her,
Can penetrate a Tiger's* armor!
Grand Science's most recent fruit
Tanks, like pike, join the pursuit!
Hardly running, slowly swimming,
Each close to each so tightly packs,
Taking the covers from their tracks,
Katyushas† move, with ripe bombs brimming.
A year ago foot-slogging mobs
Were plodding on their soles and heels!
Some imp has taught them everything
—Yes, everything!—can go on wheels!
The haughty infantry now bars

*The most powerful German tank of the latter part of the war.
†Katyusha (Katerina): nickname for multiple rocket launcher.

Переделалась на м о т о,
Бронебойки и зенитки,
Пулеметы и пожитки,
Связь и хим –, дери их прах –
Всё уселось в кузовах!
Нет пути! Дорогу ширя,
Целиной гремит в обгон
Танков Т-тридцать четыре
Бесшабашный эшелон!
Снег и землю с лязгом роет.
Мчат казаки конным строем
С красным ленточьем лампасов,
Остро вскинув плечи в бурках! –
С каждым часом, с каждым часом
К Найденбургу! к Найденбургу!

В Найденбурге рвет огонь
Добрый камень старой кладки.
Город брошен в беспорядке,
Взят в наживной лихорадке,
И, за немцами вдогон,
Тут же брошен, снова взят
Новой лавою солдат.
Ни гражданских, ни военных
Немцев нет. Но в теплых стенах
Нам оставлен весь уют –
И сквозь чад, сквозь дым, сквозь копоть,
Победители Европы,
Всюду русские снуют,

Travel in anything but cars.
Anti-aircraft, anti-tankmen,
Machine-gunners and private packs,
Signals, Chem warfare—blast them!—
Have found some corner in the trucks!
No room to pass! Right off the roadway
See the reckless squadrons broil:
T-34's are overtaking,
Rumbling through the virgin soil!
Through snow and earth they churn and clank.
Then horse-borne Cossacks, rank on rank,
Their shoulders squared back into their cloaks,
The piping along their trousers red!
—Hour by hour to Neidenburg!
Forward to Neidenburg they head!

In Neidenburg conflagrations shiver
To shards old masonry's good stone.
The town's a chaos; in a fever
Of acquisition our pursuit
Takes it, then throws it aside for one
More wave of our soldiery to share.
No Germans here in uniform
Or civvies now. But in the warm
Walls their comforts wait our care—
And through the fires, the smoke, the soot,
The Conquerors of Europe swarm,
Russians scurrying everywhere.

В кузова себе суют
Пылесосы, свечи, вина,
Трубки, юбки и картины,
Брошки, пряжки, бляшки, блузки,
Пиш-машинки не на русском,
Сыр и круги колбасы,
Мелочь утвари домашней,
Вилки, рюмки, туфли, гребни,
Гобелены и весы, —
А на ратуше, на башне,
Прорываясь в дымном небе,
Уцелевшие часы
Так же честно мерят время
Между этими и теми,
Меж приходом и уходом,
Тем же ровным-ровным ходом,
Лишь дрожат едва-едва
Древних стрелок кружева.

Стройной готики обвалы
Догорают как завалы,
Узких улиц поперек.
Пробки, сплотки и заторы,
Тем не к спеху, этим скоро, —
По ступенькам, на порог
Прут российские шоферы
Перекосом, залихватски,
Набекрень — пройдем везде!

In their trucks they stuff the loot:
Vacuum cleaners, wine and candles,
Skirts and picture frames and pipes,
Brooches, medallions, blouses, buckles,
Typewriters (not with Russian type),
Rings of sausages, and cheeses,
Small domestic ware and veils,
Combs and forks and wineglasses,
Samplers, and shoes, and scales . . .
While on the tower of the town hall,
Through a rent in the smoky sky,
The clock, surviving through it all,
Measures the time as honorably
Between the others and ourselves,
Those who've come and those who've fled,
With the same ever-even tread,
Only the ancient hands' fine lace
Is trembling slightly on its face.

Collapsing chunks of slender Gothic
Burn in an enormous mound.
Across the narrow street the traffic
Jams up solid, tightly bound:
Some too fast and some too slow—
Up steps, up thresholds, on they go,
Russian drivers batter through.
They twist and turn, devil-may-care,
At any angle, anywhere!

Мы привычны к азиатской
Тряске, ломке и езде!

Угол улиц. Кем-то встарь
Втащен, брошен здесь дикарь —
В сто пудов валун скалистый.
Из него, сечен резцом,
Выступает хмурый Бисмарк
С твердокаменным лицом.
А под Бисмарком стоит —
Чудо-юдо рыба-кит!!
Сколько едем вширь и вдоль,
Ну, такого не видали:
Вынес русским хлеб да соль —
Гля! немецкий пролетарий!
Да с салфеткой, да на блюдо.
— Что ты вылез? — Ты откуда?
— Пекарь, что ли? — Ладно, ехай!
— Он живой? А ну пошпрехай!
Может, кукла?..
          На вопросы
Распрямляется в ответ:
«Ich bin Kommunist, Genossen!
Я вас ждал двенадцать лет!..»
Лейтенант затылок чешет:
Может правда, может брешет,
Может, враг, а, может, свой,
Трать на них, собак, конвой...

We're used to Asiatic jolting,
Bumping, riding, crashing, bolting!

The crossroads. In some long-past year
Someone dragged a boulder here,
Dumped a hundred poods of granite.
Chiseled from its craggy grays,
Bismarck surlily emerges
With a stony-solid face.
And under Bismarck, see who's standing
—Well, lads, wonders never cease!—
In all the length and breadth we've traveled
We never saw the like of this!
Look! A German proletarian!
Bringing Russians bread and salt,
On a dish—and in a napkin . . .
"Where've you sprung from?" "What are you called?"
"A baker, eh?" "Come on, get moving!"
"Is he alive? Hey, sprech a bit!
A dummy, perhaps?"
                              He stands up straight
To give one answer to each question:
"Ich bin Kommunist, Genossen!
Twelve years now I've waited for you!"
The lieutenant scratches at his throat:
Perhaps he's lying, perhaps it's true.
Perhaps a friend—and then perhaps not.
Wasting guards on dogs like you . . .

– Отведите в полковой!

Фронт волною, фронт волною.
Дома в два зайти конвою,
Шкаф прошарить и столы, –
И у этой же скалы
Из седла не обернется,
Смотрит карту капитан.
А у немца сердце бьется:
«Höchste Freude!.. Rote Fahn'!..
KPD und ВКП!..»
Перевел ремень бинокля:
– Где ты взялся, будь ты проклят!
Отвести на ДивКП!
– Ну, пошел! С тобой тут, с фрицем!..

Фронт катится, фронт катится.
Тот же Бисмарк, тот же угол,
Но в сомненьи и в испуге
Угасает немца взор:
«Wenn ich könnte .. all mein Leben ..
Meine Kräfte .. ich .. soeben ..»
– Гад! Шпион! Завел молебен! –
Пишет в Виллисе майор:

"Hold him for Brigade HQ!"

Forward, forward, the front surges.
I take a squad into two houses
Rummaging through desks and cupboards—
And under the same boulder pauses
A captain; looking at his map
He sits, not turning in the saddle.
The German's heart begins to leap:
"Höchste Freude! . . . Rote Fahne!
KPD und VKP! . . ."*
The captain's pulling at the strap
Of his binoculars—"Curse you, man!
From where the hell did you spring out?
Hold him for Division, see!
Don't waste my time, just hold the Kraut!"

The front rolls on, the front rolls on.
The same Bismarck, the same boulder.
But the German's gaze grows dim,
Blinded now with doubt and terror:
"Wenn ich könnte . . . all mein Leben . . .
Meine Kräfte . . . ich . . . soeben . . ."
"Swine! Spy! What's that mumbling?"
In his jeep the major writes,

*Greatest joy! . . . Red Flag! . . . Communist Party of Germany and
All-Union Communist Party!

«СМЕРШ. С приветом. Соловьеву.
Шлю какого-то чумного.
Разберись там, оперчек,
Что за чорт за человек.»
Морщит лоб суровый Бисмарк.
Ветром дым относит быстро.
Канцлер глыбу как ковчег,
Словно взяв ее навздым,
Высоко несет сквозь дым.
И отводят коммунара
От подножья валуна.
Он кричит мне с тротуара:
«Gnädig' Herr!.. Моя жена!..
Höringstraße, zweiundzwanzig!..
Dies unwürdig' Komödie..
Я вернусь!..»
                                    Вернешься, жди..
Иностранцы, иностранцы!
Ой, по нам, младенцы вы...
Ой, не снесть вам головы...

Zweiundzwanzig, Höringstraße.
Дом не жжен, но трепан, граблен.
Чей-то стон стеной ослаблен:
Мать – не на смерть. На матрасе,
Рота, взвод ли побывал –
Дочь-девчонка наповал.

"Smersh.* With greetings. Solovyov.
I'm passing on some sort of vermin.
Field Security can determine
How to write his nonsense off."
Stern Bismarck's furrowing his forehead.
Smoke clears quickly in the breeze.
See like an ark the chancellor's boulder,
As though he sailed it through the skies
High above the drifting smoke.
Away they take the Communard
From his place below the rock,
And from the pavement's edge he cries,
"Die unwürdige Komödie!
Höringstrasse, zweiundzwanzig
—Gnäd'ger Herr! Tell my wife . . .
—I'll be back . . ."
                        Oh, wait and see . . .
You foreigners, you foreigners!
You're like babes in arms to us . . .
You really think you'll save your life? . . .

Zweiundzwanzig, Höringstrasse.
It's not been burned, just looted, rifled.
A moaning, by the walls half muffled:
The mother's wounded, still alive.
The little daughter's on the mattress,
Dead. How many have been on it?

*Smersh: Smert Shpionam (death to spies), in fact concerned in
arresting all undesirables.

Сведено к словам простым:
НЕ ЗАБУДЕМ! НЕ ПРОСТИМ!
КРОВЬ ЗА КРОВЬ и зуб за зуб!
Девку – в бабу, бабу – в труп.
Окровлён и мутен взгляд,
Просит: «Töte mich, Soldat!»
Уж темна, не видно ей:
Я – из них же, я-то чей?..
Нет для вас больниц, врачей.
Сплав стекла в местах аптек.
День сереет, тает снег...
Жил да был Parteigenosse,
Не последний и не первый,
Легший гатью под колеса,
Под колеса Коминтерна.
Русский ход державный, славься!
Мне сейчас бы трахнуть шнапса.
А еще повеселее –
Закатиться по трофеи!

На ловца и зверь бежит:

A platoon, a company perhaps?
A girl's been turned into a woman,
A woman turned into a corpse.
It's all come down to simple phrases:
Do not forget! Do not forgive!
Blood for blood!* A tooth for a tooth!
The mother begs, "Töte mich, Soldat!"†
Her eyes are hazy and bloodshot.
The dark's upon her. She can't see.
Am I one of theirs? Or whose? . . .
Doctors? Hospitals? Not for you.
Where druggists stood there's melted glass.
The day turns gray. The snow melts too . . .
Once there lived, in days now past,
A Comrade, a Parteigenosse,
Not the first and not the last
To lie prostrate, each in turn
In that log road beneath the wheels,
The wheels of the Comintern.
Russia advances, a great power.
Hail to that advance's thunder!
Some schnapps would do me good, I feel.
But what would cheer me even more—
Is to go looking for some plunder!

The wild animal runs to the hunter:‡

*Slogans issued by the Soviet High Command.
†Kill me, soldier!   ‡Russian proverb.

Мимо почты путь лежит.
Этот корпус трехэтажный
Через час огонь охватит,
А запас, запас бумажный –
Век пиши, и на век хватит!
Хоть пригладь ее щекою,
Хоть сожмурься, так бела. –
Я б с бумагою такою
Не поднялся б от стола.
Придирись, чего здесь нету,
Канцелярская душа?
Всякой жесткости и цвета
Триста три карандаша!
Не щепятся, не занозны,
Древесина их мягка,
Без усилий, грациозно
Нажимает их рука.
Кох-и-нор, почтенный Фабер,
Век Европе послужил.
Ну, а если бы теперь я
Понемножечку хотя бы –
Эти ручки, эти перья,
Эту радугу чернил
В пузырьках с притертой пробкой,
Эти сколки, скрепки, кнопки,
Папки, книжечки, коробки –
Да в машину погрузил?
Покраснею ль от стыда?

The post office, right here! Let's enter.
Within the hour the whole three-story
Block will be gulped down by fire.
Meanwhile, the stocks, the stocks of paper
—Enough to write on for a century!
Just rub it on your cheek, so smooth.
So white, it makes you screw your eyes.
—If I had paper as fine as this,
Up from my desk I'd never rise!
What's missing, what's to criticize,
You lovers of good stationery?
—Three hundred and three pencils too,
Of every hardness, every hue!
They don't crack and they don't splinter,
Their wood is beautifully soft;
Gracefully, without an effort,
The fingers close around their shaft.
Respected Fabers, Koh-i-noors,
Have served Europe a hundred years.
. . . Well, however, what do you think?
I mean, just suppose I took
A few of these pens and penholders,
This rainbow of such various ink
All in phials with ground-glass stoppers,
Paper clips, drawing pins, and scissors,
Boxes, booklets, labels, folders,
And loaded them aboard the truck?
Should I really blush for shame?

Как я жил? Бумаги гладкой
В ученической тетрадке
Я не видел никогда:
Перья рвут ее, скребут,
В грязь до дыр резинки трут;
Словно лимфа крокодила
Водянистые чернила –
И они на ней плывут.
Грифель – глина: чинишь, чинишь,
Вдруг насквозь весь грифель вынешь;
Купишь мягкий, «В», зараза, –
Режь им стекла как алмазом.
И мертвеет вдохновенье,
Мысль роняешь камнем ко дну, –
Как же мне без восхищенья
В этот зал войти сегодня?
Как искатель кладов рыщет,
Обезумев по пещерам,
Так хожу здесь алчный, нищий,
Лишь одетый офицером.
Уж теперь, когда пришел к ним,
Только пальцами прищелкну:
То – забрать! и это – тоже!
Перед кем краснеть я должен?
Я б указчика такого
Да послал пожить в Союзе.
– Старшина! Вот это всё вот

What was the life I led before?
Smooth paper in an exercise book
Was something that I never saw.
Ours our pens would scratch and tear,
Erasers made dirty marks and holes.
The ink was just a watery slop
Like lymph produced from crocodiles,
With black specks floating on the top.
The pencils were some sort of clay.
Yes, you'd sharpen, sharpen away,
And suddenly the whole lead's gone.
Or buy a soft B pencil—curse!
Diamond-hard, it would cut glass.
Your inspiration drops down dead,
Your thought sinks in the depths like stone.
So, now into these halls I've come,
With admiration I'm struck dumb.
As a treasure seeker searches,
Near insane, through endless caves,
Just dressed up as an officer
In me a greedy pauper raves.
So now I'm where they had it stored, I
Snap my fingers, give an order:
"That's to go . . . that too . . . that too!"
Who should I blush in front of? Who?
Anyone who points the finger
—Go live in the U.S.S.R.!
"Sergeant major! All this pile here,

Пусть ребята грузят в кузов!

А пока тащат да валят,
Узкой улкой нам в обгон
В дымке смеси, в лязге стали
Мчится танков эшелон.
А пока мотор заводят,
Левым боком нас обходят,
Чтоб поспеть подальше к ночи,
Всё, что взято – приторочив,
Бросив всё, что не с руки,
Удоволены победой
И гулянкой, и обедом,
Ухмыляясь, казаки.
В нашей жизни беспокойной –
Нынче жив, гляди – убит, –
Мил мне, братцы, ваш разбойный
Не к добру веселый вид.
Выбирали мы не сами,
Не по воле этот путь,
Но теперь за поясами
Есть чем по небу пальнуть!
Так не зря же! Так не жаль же!
Худо-бедно наверстаем!
Скачем дальше! катим дальше!
В Алленштайн! в Алленштайн!!

Have the lads load it in the car!"

They cram it in. And rolling fast
Down the narrow street in file,
With smoke of engines, clank of steel,
A tank squadron presses past.
We start the engine. Cossacks ride
Agallop down the left-hand side,
On and on till the fall of night.
Strapped to their mounts they've kept the best
Loot, and thrown away the rest;
And merry, full of satisfaction,
With all the victories they're winning
—And the boozing, and the feasting,
They sweep past us, grinning, grinning.
Our lives don't see much relaxation.
Alive? Watch out or you'll be dead!
By your cheerful brigand faces
—So sinister—I'm comforted.
This road was not our own decision.
No one asked us if or why.
But now under our belts we've something
Worth a salvo in the sky!
It's not in vain! There's no regretting!
We'll settle up! We'll manage fine!
And so, let's gallop! Let's keep rolling!
To Allenstein! To Allenstein!

Алленштайн только взят,
Взят внезапно час назад
Конно-танковым ударом,
Ни сплошным еще пожаром,
Ни разгулом не объят.
Домы полны. Немцы в страхе,
Запершись в ночном тепле,
Стука ждут в тревожной мгле.
Ночь горит: горящий сахар –
Фиолетовое пламя! –
Растекает по земле.
Дрожь огней, лиловый трепет!
Льет из склада меж домами
Чай шальной,что нами не пит.
Если в валеных сапожках,
Обходи кругом, Митрошка,
Обходи шагов за сто!
Не смотря, что снег растоплен,
Два узбека в луже с воплем
За вечернее манто
Ухватились, уцепились,
Не уступят ни за что.
Свет лилов, лиловым мехом
Отливает. На потеху
Третий, русский, закричал им:
«Погоди! Обоим дам!» –
Подскочил к ним и кинжалом
Перерезал пополам.
В кой бы дом искать добычу?
Где богаче? где верней?
Ванька в дверь прикладом тычет,

Allenstein has just been taken.
An hour ago, a sudden strike
Of tanks and cavalry overwhelmed it.
It's not engulfed yet in the thick
Of raging troops and total fire.
Full houses. Germans lurk in fear
In the warm night, behind their locks.
In anxious gloom they await our knocks.
Now the night flares. Burning sugar:
It flames with violet-colored fire!
Over the earth it seems to simmer,
A trembling blaze, a lilac shimmer.
Out of the warehouse see it pour
Like some strange tea we won't be drinking.
—If your boots are made of felt,
Keep a good hundred paces clear,
Mitroshka! The snow starts to melt.
Two Uzbeks howling in a puddle
They haven't noticed yet, fight on.
They've grabbed, and neither will let go of,
An evening cloak: they won't back down.
The light has turned a furry lilac.
A Russian soldier, for a laugh,
Shouts, "Here, now, both of you can have it!"
His bayonet slices it in half.
—In which house to seek the loot?
Which is richer? Which is safer?
Vanka bangs with his rifle butt,

Глядь – а Дунька из дверей! –
Что по туфлям, по зачёсу,
Джемпер, юбочка, ну – немка!
Тем лишь только, что курноса,
Распознаешь своеземку.
Руки в боки, без испуга
Прислонилась к косяку.
«Кто ты есть?» – «А я – прислуга.»
«Будет врать-то земляку!
Ни подола, чтоб захлюстан,
Ни сосновых башмаков, –
Пропусти!»
　　　　　 – «Да кто ж тя пустит?
Пьяный, грязный, тьфу каков!»
К парню – новые солдаты,
Девка речь ведет иначе:
«Погодите-ка, ребяты!
Покажу вам дом богаче!
Немок-целок полон дом!»
«Чай далеко?»
　　　　　　　 «За углом!
Потружусь уж, покажу,
Как землячка, послужу!»
Дверь захлопнув за собою,
Налегке перед толпою
Убегает, их маня
В свете синего огня.
За углом исчезли круто,
Стуки, звоны и возня,
И еще через минуту
Где-то тут же, из-за стенки,
Крик девичий слышен только:

And look—it's Dunka come to answer.
Judged by her hairdo and her shoes,
Her skirt and jumper—she's a German!
And it's only by her snub nose
One spots a fellow countrywoman.
She leans against the doorpost there,
Unafraid, with hands on hips.
"Who are you, then?" "I'm the servant."
"Don't tell lies to your own chaps!
You're not in clogs. Your skirt is clean.
Let me in!"
      "What? Let you in?
A drunken, dirty . . ." Other soldiers
Come up. She takes a different tone:
"Wait, lads, I'll show you something finer,
A rich house, full of German virgins!"
"Far away?"
      "Just around the corner!
You'll see! I'll serve you like a good
Fellow countrywoman should!
I'll show you!" The door goes slam.
Away she runs, ahead of them,
Lightly, leading the crowd, she goes,
Lit up by the bluish blaze.
Around the corner they disappear.
Knocks. Rings. A tumult. Then we hear
A moment later, the cry of a girl,
Somewhere, from behind a wall,

«Я не немка! Я не немка!!
Я же – полька!! Я же полька...»
Шебаршат единоверцы,
Кто что схватит, где поспеет, –
　　　«Ну, какое сердце
　　　Устоять сумеет?!..»

Алленштайновский вокзал
Только-только принимал
Пассажиров, кто бежал
Вглубь, в Германию, на запад,
И о том, что он внезапно
В руки русские попал,
Там, восточнее, не знают,
Отправляют, отправляют
Мирных жителей сюда,
Женщин, девушек-беглянок,
Малых, старых поезда,
И соседний полустанок –
Расхлестнувшийся, туда
Не дошел передний край –
Перед каждым эшелоном
В черном лаке телефона
Слышит мерно: «Strecke frei»
«Strecke frei» – весь бой, весь вечер,
Ночь до утра шлет им, шлет им
Алленштайновский диспетчер –

"I'm not German! I'm not German!
No! I'm—Polish! I'm a Pole! . . ."
Grabbing what comes handy, those
Like-minded lads get in and start—
            "And, oh, what heart
                Could well oppose? . . ."

The railway station of Allenstein
Till now accepted down the line
The fleeing passengers who pressed
Into Germany, to the west.
Out to the east there's ignorance
That it's fallen so suddenly
Into the hands of the enemy.
Train after train they keep on sending
Of peaceable inhabitants:
Women, young girl refugees,
The very young, the very old.
And every time, the nearby halt
—A place the front has not yet reached—
Still confused, misunderstanding,
Before train after train's dispatched,
Hears always the regular
"Strecke frei!"* from the phone's black lacquer.
"Strecke frei!" through battle, through dusk,
Through the night, till dawn, he sends it on
—The Allenstein dispatcher—not an

*The line is clear.

Не чужой, не русский, – свой!
Немец! в светлых каплях пота
Затаенный, восковой,
Ходит роботом. Пред ним,
Выпыхая черный дым,
За столом – майор огромный,
Службы общевойсковой,
Обожженный, смуглый, темный,
С пышной черной бородой, –
   Саблю – на стол,
   Ноги – на стул,
В голевом тулупе белом.
Спирт, сопя, из фляжки хлещет.
Выпьет – взглянет осовело.
Перетянут, перекрещен,
Грозен, зол, не жди добра,
На боку в распах, зловеще,
Пистолета кобура.
У майора ординарец
Расторопен образцово:
Опростав походный ларец
На пол зала изразцовый,
Мебель шашкой нащепя,
Оглянулся вкруг себя –
И костер повеселу
Вот уж брызжет на полу.
Котелки и сковородки –
Всё шипит в порядке четком,
И д о м а ш н и е консервы

Alien Russian but one of their own!
A German! His face a waxen mask,
Melting in paler drops of sweat,
He moves like a robot. Opposite,
Puffing out black clouds of smoke,
Sits a huge General Service major,
Hardened, sallow-skinned, and dark,
With a beard of black luxuriant hair—
    On the table—his saber,
    His feet—on the chair,
In a greatcoat with white sheepskin lining.
Raw alcohol from a flask he's draining.
He'll drink, and out of his torpor stare,
In his cross-strapping and his belt,
He's bitter, ferocious, ominous,
Ill-meant, under his open coat,
The holster of his pistol shows.
The major has an orderly
—A model of efficiency.
He empties out the field canteen
Onto the tiling of the floor,
And then, with blows of his own saber,
Starts to chop up the furniture.
Soon a bonfire's blazing ready,
Sputtering cheerfully on the tiles,
The mess tins and the frying pans
—In good order it all boils.
Soon the water's seething hot.
See the *homemade* dainties quicken:

Оживают в кипятке,
И вторая вслед за первой
Тонет к у р к а в чугунке.
Парень весел, хлопец вражий,
Напевает, стопку в раже
Опрокинет налету, —
И порхают хлопья сажи
В электрическом свету.
Доглядясь сквозь дым махорки,
Вижу я: майор не спит, —
Мутен, пьян, устал, но зорко
За диспетчером следит.
А диспетчер, сгорбясь зябло,
Опершись о стол ослабло,
Путь и поезд пишет в книгах,
В перезвонах, в перемигах
Ламп, сигналов и звонков,
　　　　Как привычно,
　　　　Механично
Аккуратен и толков,
Эшелоны принимая,
Одноземцев отправляя
В жизнь иную, в ад и в рай,
Мерной фразой «Strecke frei».
В час четырежды по зданью
Отдаются содроганьем
Тяжесть мощных паровозов,

First one and then another chicken
Sinks into the waiting pot.
A cheerful boy, a hostile bastard:
In a rage he's humming, muttering,
As he knocks back a shot of booze,
And the flakes of soot are fluttering
Up through the electric blaze.
Through thick makhorka* smoke I'm peering,
And see the major's not asleep.
Dulled, drunk, he's able still to keep
A sharp eye on the trapped dispatcher.
And the dispatcher, ever-wearying,
At the table slumped and wilting,
Writes trains and routes into his ledger,
Accepting carriages and trucks
In sequences of ringing, blinking
Lamp and signal and bell,
      Just as usual,
      Quite mechanical,
Reliably, meticulously,
Sending his fellow countrymen
To a new life—hell or heaven,
With the flat phrase "Strecke frei."
And so it is, four times an hour,
The station building shakes and strains
With the weight of powerful engines,

*Coarse Russian tobacco.

Поездов катящих дрожь.

А майор совсем не грозен.
Доглядеться – он похож
На дворнягу: добродушен,
В лохмах черных. Заломя,
Насторожил шапки уши,
И одно торчит торчмя.
Душ распахнутый простор! –
Фронт! Как будто с давних пор
Мы знакомы – руку, руку!
Ты – куда? откуда? – я?
Я – звукач, ловлю по звуку,
Да не слышно ни...
– Штаба фронта, из Седьмого.
Разложенье войск противных.
– А! про вас историй дивных
Я наслышан. Сам с к а к о г о?
Где бывал?
               – Под Руссой.
                     – Ловать?
– Как? И ты?
               – Ну да, и мы
С первых месяцев зимы.
– Генка! Кружки! Выпить повод!
Это ж редкостный земляк!
А Осташков?..
               – Бор, Марёво..
Церковь, горка и овраг?

Vibration of the rolling trains.

The major's not ferocious really.
Looked at closer, he's more like
An amiable and even-tempered,
Black, curly-coated mongrel tyke.
He pricks up the earflaps of his hat:
One of them sticks right up straight.
The Front! Free territory for minds!
It's as though we've been acquainted
For ages. We hold out our hands.
"Where are you from?" "Where you headed?"
A sound ranger, I pinpoint by sounds.
"I'm sorry, I didn't quite catch the . . ."
"Front Staff: Seventh Section
—Demoralization of the Enemy."
"I've heard strange stories of your crew!
Which was your unit? In what action?"
"Near Russa."
            "Lovat?"
                    "What, you too?"
"The first months of that winter. Yes!"
"Genka! Mugs! We'll drink to this!
A chap from the same parts! It's rare!
—And Ostashkov? . . ."
                    "Bor, Marevo . . .
The church, that hill, the gully there?"

– Лупачиха?

          – Озерище..

– Где потом?

          – Орел.

                    – Дружище!

Становой Колодезь?

                    – Ляды!

Мы же были...

               – Мы же рядом!

Лютый Корень!

                – Русский Брод!

Зуша!

     – Чаполоть!

               – Заплот!

– Мост и ров... Да ты присядь!

Генка! Скоро там пожрать?..

Я – з а п а с.

          – И я – з а п а с.

Где бы к а д р а м, entre nous,

Без запасников, без нас,

Эту б выиграть войну!

Кем был д о?

            В косматой шкуре,

В гуле гибнущей земли:

– Я – доцент литературы

Из московского ИФЛИ.

– Из МИФЛИ?!

             Без шапки...

                     – Ба!

Я вас видел там! Судьба!

"Lupachikha?"

       "Ozerische . . ."

"Where next?"

       "Orel."

             "A friend! A friend!

Stanovoi Kolodez?"

       "Lyadi!

Why, we were . . ."

        "We were close at hand!

Lyuti Koren!"

       "Russki Brod!

Zusha!"

     "Chapolot!"

       "Zaplot!"

"Bridge, anti-tank ditch . . . take a seat!

Genka! The grub's not ready yet?

I'm a reservist."

       "Yes, me too.

Well, without us, *entre nous*,

How would the regulars win this war!

—What was it that you did *before?*"

In the shaggy skin, as around him sweeps

The rumbling of a world's collapse:

"I'm a lecturer in literature

At the Moscow IFLI Institute."

"MIFLI!

     Hats off to you! Why, sure!

Of course, I met you there! It's fate!

Только эта борода
Не росла у вас тогда.
— С сорок первого. С обетом —
Не сбривать до дня Победы.
— На лице не помню шрама.
— Ильмень-озеро. Раненье.
В ярком верхнем освещеньи
Узнаю, каков был там он:
«Век великий Просвещенья!
Век Вольтера! Век Бентама!»
Мудрецов по стенам лики.
У студенток трепет век.
«Восемнадцатый, великий,
Человеком гордый век!»
Помню, помню! Свеж, разглажен,
Остроумен, оживлен,
Вёрток, прост, непринужден,
В смелых выводах отважен,
Красноречием палим,
За звонок читал, и даже
Коридором шли за ним.
А теперь отяжелели,
Разжирели я и он,
Еле-еле, еле-еле
Набираем мы разгон —
И взахлёб, бесперебойно,
Торопливо, беспокойно,
Пьем ли, курим ли, едим —

The beard's the only change one sees,
You hadn't grown it in those days."
"From 1941. —I swore
I'd not shave till we'd won the war."
"Your face—I don't recall the scar."
"A wound—on the Lake Ilmen front."
Under the high lantern's glare
I remember him back there:
"The Great Age—the Enlightenment!
The age of Bentham! Of Voltaire!"
Walls hung with pictures of the wise.
Girl students fluttering their eyes.
"In the great eighteenth century,
Proud only of humanity!"
I recollect, I recollect!
Fresh-faced, animated, witty,
Relaxed and subtle and direct,
Daring in his bold conclusions,
On fire with his own eloquence,
He lectured on after the bell
—We'd even follow him down the hall.
But now we're both a little heavy,
We're fatter, gone a bit to seed.
Our conversation, stiff and awkward,
Starts at last to gather speed.
We stumble on in haste. There's no
Interruption. Anxious, quick,
Drinking, smoking, eating now,

Говорим и говорим.
Книгам клич! Сейчас он царь их,
Он — на память в их строках.
Жизнь живая блещет в карих
Протрезвившихся глазах.
Трижды клятые вопросы —
Русь, монголы и Европа —
Расстегнулся, шапку сбросил,
Чуток, тонок, мягок, тёпел.
Будто грудь его дыханьем
Разорвала тесный обруч,
Говорит он о Германьи
Понимающий и добрый, —
Но разведенные плечи
Высоко несут погоны,
И — лунатиком диспетчер
Принимает эшелоны.

И — казаки по вагонам.
Звон от сабель. Стук прикладов.
«Вы-ходи!» И по перрону
В шубках, в шляпках, в ботах, стадом —
«Без вещей, как есть!» — бессильных
Перепуганных ц и в и л ь н ы х
Всех пешком на пункты сбора
Снегом розовым сквозь город,
Отбивая по пути,
С кем вольно им провести
В подворотне, там ли, тут,

We talk and talk and talk and talk . . .
A call to books! He's now their Tsar,
He has their pages in his heart!
—Essential life is sparkling out
Of hazel, newly sobered eyes.
The thrice-accursed questions rise—
Old Rus, the Mongols, Europe . . . And,
Unbuttoning, throwing off his hat,
He's turning sensitive, subtle, kind,
As though a deep inhaling burst
Some tight hoop around his chest:
He speaks even of Germany
With understanding, with sympathy.
But on his broad, well-flung-back shoulder,
The high proud epaulette remains,
And—in a trance there the dispatcher
Still goes on accepting trains.

And . . . Cossacks go from carriage to carriage.
Sabers ring and rifles thud.
"O-u-t!" And down along the platform
In fur coats, hats, and boots they herd—
"Leave your things!" They drive the helpless
Terrified *civilians* now
On foot to the collection depot
Across the town, through rosy snow.
On the way, they start selecting
Those they feel they want to spend a

Вгоряче пяток минут.
Генерал из интендантов
С одинарцем, с адьютантом,
Ходит с палочкой, хромой,
Остриём, ее, как щупом,
Чуть брезгливо между трупов
Отбирая, что домой.
И едва укажет стэком
Шарфик, перстень, туфли, ткань ли, —
Взято вподхвать челаэком,
Утонуло в чемодане.
Чемоданов с ними три,
Всё поместится внутри.
Буйной ярмарки товары
По платформам, по путям —
С пылу, с жару, шаром-даром
Разбирай ко всем чертям! —
Две корзины венских булок,
Узел дамского, грехи,
Сигареты из Стамбула
И французские духи!
Ну, беда, куда всё денешь?
Шелкова́ белья наденешь
Восемь пар, шинелка туго.
Солдатня столпилась кругом
У покинутой коляски,
      Голубой,
      Да кружевной:

Hot five minutes with in a doorway
Or any corner that comes handy.
A limping general from Supply,
With orderly and ADC,
Just a shade distastefully,
Picks his way among the corpses,
Choosing stuff for sending home.
Probing with his stick, he shows
A scarf, a ring, some cloth, some shoes.
And at once they're seized and sunk
In the black depths of a trunk.
They've three trunks. The lad can work it—
Everything will fit inside.
It's all like some tumultuous market
Along the platform and the road.
For no reason, on an impulse,
Take what you like, by all the devils!
Two baskets of Vienna rolls,
—What sins—a pile of ladies' wear,
Cigarettes from Istanbul,
And French perfume . . . The trouble's where
One's going to stow it all. All right,
You put silk underclothes on—well,
Eight sets, and your coat's too tight.
Some soldiers have gathered around
A pram that's been abandoned,
                              Blue,
        Lace trimmings too:

«Вот – младенец.
Он ведь немец!
Подрастет – наденет каску.
Рассчитать его теперь?
Есть приказ Верховной Ставки!..
КРОВЬ ЗА КРОВЬ!»
        – «По пьяной лавке
Говоришь или стрезва?
Сам ты Ирод, поп твой зверь!»
«Дед! Не я ведь! Дед! – Москва!»

«По машинам!» Снова в путь.
Ни вздремнуть, ни отдохнуть.
Как в цветном калейдоскопе,
Катим, катим по Европе,
От бессонницы, от хмеля
Окрылели, осмелели.
Всё смешалось, всё двоится –
Перекрестки, стрелки, лица,
Взрывы, встречи, мины, раны,
Страхи, радость, зло, добро,
Прусских ночек свет багряный,
Прусских полдней серебро.
То шоссе, то вперекрест
Две слеги, и все в объезд.
Путь меняет рок железный.
Проплывает, как во сне:

"Look, a little 'un.
        Still, he's a German!
He'll grow and put a helmet on.
Deal with him now, d'you think?
The order from Supreme Command
Is *Blood for Blood! Give no quarter!*"
"To talk like that! What, are you drunk?
Are you Herod? Is your priest
Some abominable beast?"
"It's not me, grandpa!—Moscow's order!"

"Board!" Forward the column goes
Once more. No time to rest or doze.
We roll on and on over Europe
As in a strange kaleidoscope.
From lack of sleep and drunkenness
We've turned daring, we've grown wings.
Everything's mixed up, everything's
Double—crossroads, signposts, faces,
Explosions, meetings, wounds, and mines,
Evil and good, fears and delights,
The silver of the Prussian noons,
The crimson of the Prussian nights.
Two logs stand crossed upon the road
To signal detour. Iron fate's
Changed its route. Dreamlike there floats
Before us, somewhere to the side,
Silent, trackless, deep in snows,

Где-то в тихой, непроездной
Заснеженной стороне
Чей-то дом уединенный,
Лес нетронутый за ним,
Чья-то шумная колонна
На печной свернула дым.
Чуть моторы заглуша,
Греться спешились, спеша.
Вкруг спины колотят зябло,
В дом! Хохочут: «М а т к а, я й к и!»
И подносит им хозяйка
Наливных сквозистых яблок.
Расхватали, походили.
Меж зубов морозный похруст.
Дай хозяйку застрелили,
Пух ковра обрызгав вó кровь,
Муж в кровати – долечили
Автоматом заодно.
Лишь мальчонок, их внучонок,
Умелькнул, раскрыл окно,
За забор, прыжок! прыжок!
      Как зверенок,
      Как зайченок
Полем к лесу наутёк,
Уклоняясь и юля;
Вслед с дороги чуть не взвод,
Беспорядочно паля:

Someone's solitary house,
With the virgin woods behind.
Someone's noisy column turned
Toward smoke rising from the hearth.
They've hardly cut the engines' noise
When they're out to find some warmth.
Slapping their shoulders, they reach the house.
Now they're in. She stands there, numb.
They laugh. "Get us some eggs then, mum!"
And the housewife does her best,
Brings them apples, ripe and brittle,
They grabbed them, walked around a little,
A crunch between their teeth like frost.
And then they shot the housewife first,
Spattering with blood the carpet's pile.
The husband was bedridden, ill:
They cured him with a carbine burst.
Only the grandson, a young boy,
In a flash managed to escape
—Out of the window and away
Over the fence with a leap! With a leap!
        Like a wild creature,
        Like a little hare,
Across the field toward the wood
Running, ducking, dodging aside.
The whole troop, nearly, rushed from the road,
Firing anyhow, in pursuit:

— На спор! — Ранен! — Есть! — Уйдет!
   — На-ка! На-ка!
     Ах, собака,
Убежал. Ну, подрастет...

В свете солнца больно глянуть:
Поле снежное искряно,
Ни слединки колеса.
В пухе снега, в блестках льдяных
Безмятежные леса.
Там, у нас, по русской шири
Фронт стоял, и нет лесов,
Осталась сплошная вырубь
От военных топоров.
Блиндажи перекрывали
Наших сосенок стволы.
Жалко, здесь не воевали —
Ишь, стоят горды, белы,
Русской нет на них пилы!..
Синим льдом сверкнут озера,
Белизной увиты реки.
В селах — дуб комодов, шторы,
Пианино и камины,
Радио, библиотеки.
Словно путь проспектом Невским —
В каждом доме Достоевский,
Полный, розный, а в одном

"I'll get him!" "Winged him!" "He's down!"
"He's away!" "—Shoot! Shoot!"
"Ah, the brute,
    He's got away. Well, when he's grown . . ."

It hurts to gaze through the sun's sheen;
The snowy field sparkles aglow.
There's not a wheel track to be seen.
Under shining ice, in a dust of snow,
The forests stretch quietly away.
Back there in our Russian spaces
Where the front was, the woods have gone.
Miles and miles of stumps remain:
Army axes cut them down.
We used the trunks of our own pines
To build the bunkers of our lines.
This would have been the place to fight—
See them standing, proud and white,
And there's no Russian saw to fell them! . . .
The lakes are sparkling with blue ice,
The rivers wrapped in whitenesses.
And in the villages, the shutters,
The oak cupboards, the things that fill them,
The pianos and the fireplaces,
The radios and the libraries.
The road's a real Nevsky Prospect—
Dostoevsky—not a house without him:
The Works, odd volumes—once, in fact,

Даже рукопись о нем.

Нам навстречу понемногу
Оживляются дороги.
Итальянцы, дай бог ноги,
Из союзной им земли
Так же голы, как пришли,
О добытке не тревожась,
На морозе жимко ёжась,
Каблучишками стучат,
Скалят зубы и кричат,
Машут русским в честь победы.
Р-разбегайся по домам,
Рим, Неаполь и Милан!
Увязав велосипеды
Кой-каким подручным грузом,
Предприимчиво французы
Крутят, отбыв вражий плен,
На Париж и на Амьен.
Не теряйся, молодцы!
В синем, в рыжем и в зеленом
Валят сбродом возбужденным.
Пан усатый под уздцы
Фуру горкою спускает,
Через верх нагружена,
Холст трофеи прикрывает,
И лицо от нас скрывает,
Застыдясь, его жена.

Even a manuscript about him.

The roads are beginning to come to life,
They're moving toward us, gradually.
The Italians now—God give them legs—
Are leaving the land of their ally
—Leaving as naked as they came,
Not bothering to stop off for loot
Huddled up, shivering in the frost
—But now they bare their teeth and shout,
Their silly heels clack. They wave away
To the Russians, in honor of victory.
The order is "S-scatter! Go back home
To Naples and Milan and Rome!"
Whirling along on their bicycles,
With curious hand luggage tied on firm,
The French, the enterprising French,
Having finished their prisoner term,
For Paris, Amiens . . . each one heads,
Ah, well, don't you get lost, brave lads!
And so, in blue and green and drab,
They pour along, an excited mob.
A mustachioed Pole is holding his bridle
As his wagon rolls down a little hill;
It's piled until it's nearly bursting:
With a canvas sheet he's covered the spoil.
But, look, his wife seems a little embarrassed—
When she sees us she turns her face away.

Видно Машку под платочком
И на козлах у поляка.
– Эй, краса! молодка! дочка!
Ты куда же?

            – Мы под Краков.
– Ай, девчонка, ходим с нами!
Забодает ведь усами!..
Мир кружится каруселью,
В семь небес пылит веселье,
Всем на свете прощено,

      Но...
Строем зачем-то шагают виновно
Русские. Пленные. Безостановно.
Спины промечены едкими метками.
Это клеймо не затравишь ничем.
Лиху дорожку под сниклыми ветками
Топчут, задумавшись сами: зачем?
К пиру не прошены, к празднику не

                       званы,
В мире одни никому не нужны,
Будто склонясь под топорное лезвие,
Движутся к далям жестокой страны.

Немцев долгие обозы
Из фургонов перекрытых
Вдоль дорог скрипят, скрипят,
Наступленьем нашим грозным
Где-то северней отбиты
И повернуты назад.

But under the scarf we can see it's a Russian
Woman who sits on the Polack's dray.
"Hey, little daughter! Where are you heading?"
"Down near Cracow."
                    "Oh, Mashka! You peach!
We're the ones you should go with, darling!
He'll gore you to death with that mustache!" . . .
—The universe spins like a roundabout.
Festivity flames to the seventh heaven.
Everyone in the world's forgiven.
        But . . .
See in formation—with a guilty look—
March Russians. Prisoners. Endless. On each back
Brand of a flame that no atonement quenches.
They tramp the hard path under hanging branches.
And always "Why?" their thought runs on and on.
They've not been summoned to the celebration,
And to our feasts they've had no invitation.
So they, alone in all the world unwanted,
Move forward, their necks bowed as though to bend
Under the harsh stroke of a clumsy ax blade,
Toward the distant parts of a cruel land.

And now in various covered wagons,
Lumbering on with squeaks and groans,
Come disoriented Germans,
Somewhere northward intercepted
By our terrible advance.

Под брезента долгий болок
Скрывши утварь и семью,
У развилка на проселок,
Сбочь шоссейной, на краю,
Терпеливо ждут просвета
В нескончаемом потоке,
Цепенея перед этой
Силой, грянувшей с востока,
И, безвольные к защите,
Прячут голову меж плеч,
Грабь их, бей их, подойди ты,
Чтоб коней у них отпречь.
Но, насытясь в наступленьи,
Как по долгу службы, с ленью
Теребят их захоронки
Наши парни, ковко, звонко
Проходя дорогой торной.
Взять — оно бы не зазорно,
Да ведь возят барахло,
А в п о с ы л к у — пять кило...
Всюду женщины — в обозе,
Под тряпьем в любом возке,
Разордевшись на морозе,
Нам навстречу налегке
По две, несколько. Одна,
Белокура и пышна,
Распрямясь, идет не робко
Вдоль шоссе по крайней тропке

Family, possessions too, in
Sledges, under tight tarpaulin.
Where the country side road stops
At the fork into the highway,
They wait patiently for gaps
In our endless stream of troops.
And their blood runs ever colder
At the might out of the East.
The will to defend themselves is lost:
They hide their face down in their shoulder.
Beat them! Steal their horses! Rob! . . .
—But, sated with loot in the advance,
Lazily doing a routine job,
Our lads just rummage through their stock
Noisily, ostentatiously,
Following the beaten track.
Take your choice. No need to blush . . .
But they're carrying worthless trash,
And the limit for sending home's
No more than five kilograms.
And everywhere women—in the line of carts,
Or under cloth in a closed sledge,
Their faces reddening in the frost.
Some come towards us without luggage
In twos and threes. And then we see
One, blond and magnificent,
Stride erect and quite unshyly
Along the path beside the highway,

С несклоненной головой
В рыжей шубке меховой,
В шапке-вязанке с портфелем.
Чуть минует с осторожкой
В туфле маленькою ножкой
Занесенные трофеи,
Где укрыто, где торчит
В небо четверо копыт.
Мы – в заторе. По две, по три
В ряд машины. Кто прыжком
Греет ноги, кто бежком.
Глаз не прячет, смело смотрит,
Каждым взглядом нам дерзя,
Будто взять ее нельзя.
На подвижном белом горле
Вро́спашь меха – шарф цветной.
С батареей нас затерло,
И в машине головной –
Opelblitz из Wehrmacht'а
Плавный ход и формы гнуты,
Утонув в сиденьи мягком,
В полушубок я закутан.
Чуть щекочет шею шёрстка..
Чтоб не спать – сосу конфетки.
Светит зелено двухвёрстка
В целлулоиде планшетки.
Я и вижу и не вижу,
Как подходит немка ближе,

Keeping her proud head unbent.
With a briefcase, in a reddish fur coat,
With small shoes and a knitted hat,
With a little care she neatly misses
All the litter of foul trophies—
Here they're decently covered, there
Four hooves stick up into the air.
We're in a traffic jam, two or three
Vehicles deep. It's getting colder.
Some men are jumping up and down
To warm their feet, and others run.
She looks bold, with her gaze up high,
As if daring us, with a bright eye,
Just as though we'd not assault her.
Around the mobile white throat
A colored scarf's under her coat.
—We're all entangled with the guns,
And in the lead vehicle packed
—An Opelblitz from the Wehrmacht,
How smooth it looks, how well it runs—
I'm sunk in a comfortable seat,
Bundled in a sheepskin coat:
Its wool scarcely tickles my throat . . .
I'm sucking sweets, so as not to sleep.
And in its case the large-scale map
Through the talc is glowing greenly.
I both see and do not see
How the German girl draws nearer,

Как, солдат завидя, шаг
Убыстряет свой и как,
Колыхнув большой фигурой,
Ничего не говоря,
К ней шагнул сержант Батурин,
Цвет-блатняга, на Амуре
Отбывавший лагеря.
С ним и Сомин напряженно
Подошел и приглушенно
Приказал: «А дай-ка пóртфель!»
Так же выпрямленно-гордо
Стала. «Что там? Покажи-ка!»
Густо краска разошлась.
Расстегнула и как выкуп
Протянула: «Bitte, Schnaps».
В литр бутылка. А налито
Треть ли, четверть ли от литра.
Чуть скосясь на Untermensch'ей
Ждет струной, в румянце. Раса!
Жду, сощурясь — не возьмут ли? —
Грамм по триста в день, не меньше,
Из возимого запаса
Выдаю. Батурин мутно
Глянул, руку протянул, —
Сомин — хвать, и как гранату
В снег нетронутый швырнул.
«Низко русского солдата
Ценишь, девка!»
                              И портфель
Вырвал, вытряхнул — сорочка,

And how, when she sees our men,
She starts to speed her pace—and then
Heaving his enormous frame,
Sergeant Baturin, flower of crime,
Ex-convict who had served his time
In labor camp on the Amur,
Strode unspeaking up to her.
Somin went over, tense and bitter,
And ordered her, in a muffled voice,
"Come on—that briefcase. Hand it over!"
She stood proud and erect as ever.
"Well, what have you got there? Show us!"
The color spread thickly through her face.
Out of her case she took a bottle,
And held it like ransom: "Bitte, schnapps."
Not full: a quarter—a third, perhaps—
Had gone already. She looked a little
Askance at the Untermenschen there.
String-taut, flushed, she waited. Race!
I wait, screw my eyes up. Will they settle?
I issue three hundred grams, not less,
A daily ration, brought up by Supply.
Baturin looked dully; his hands went forward.
—But Somin grabbed at it like a grenade
And hurled it right in the untouched snow.
"Young woman, you seem to have a low
Opinion of Russia's soldiery!"
He snatched the briefcase, shaking free

Гребни, письма и платочки,
Фотокарточек мятель…

Предо мной — газета, карта,
Отмечаю ход фронтов:
Если здесь и здесь удар, то
В феврале мы здесь, а в марте…
«Что тебе?» Суров, без слов,
Сомин мне в окно кабины
Фотоснимок подает —
Взгляд надменный; снят мужчина;
В форме; с лоском; оборот:
«Meiner innigst g'liebten Braut
In dem Tag… im Garten, wo…»

— Ну, так что ж? Отдай ей. Право,
Я не вижу ничего.
— Как, а свастика?
                            — Да, верно,
Нарукавник.
                      — Так жених
Из SS?
            — SS, наверно…
Черт их знает, как у них…
И — махнул рукой на миг…
Знак, орел, сукна окраска, —
Кой их леший разберет,
Что такую же повязку
Arbeitsdienst носил и Todt.
Что-то дрогнуло в заторе,
Заработали моторы,

A shirt, combs, letters, and handkerchiefs
—And a snowstorm of photographs.

I look at a newspaper and maps.
I'm marking the progress of the front.
If we strike here and here, perhaps
In February, March . . . "What do you want?"
Somin hands sternly, without a word,
Through the car window, a photograph
—Of a man, arrogant and stiff,
Uniformed, glossily turned out.
And on the back the writings show:
"Meiner innigst g'liebten Braut
An dem Tag . . . im Garten, wo . . ."

"What about it? Give it back to her.
I don't see anything . . ."
                              "The swastika!"
"True . . ." "And so the fiancé's
In the SS?" "I suppose he is . . .
The devil knows what it means to them . . ."
I give a quick wave of my hand.
Symbol, eagle, colored band—
What wood demon could sort them out?
What of the Arbeitsdienst and Todt
Insignia, don't they wear the same?
Something stirred in the traffic jam.
Our engines began revving up.

И, уже снимаясь с места,
Я увидел: от невесты
Сделал Сомин шаг назад,
Снял Батурин автомат
И – не к ней, а от нее! –
Тело выбросил свое.
Без сговора, полукругом,
Словно прячась друг за другом,
Шаг за шагом, три, четыре,
Молча, дальше, шире, шире –
Что? Зачем? Собрать нагнулась –
     – Оглянулась –
       Поняла! –
Завизжала, в снег упала
И комочком замерла
Как зверок недвижный, желтый...
Автомат еще не щелкал
     Миг. Другой.
Я! – зачем махнул рукой?!
      Боже мой!
     Машина! стой!
    «Эй! ребята!..»
     Автоматы –
Очередь. И по местам...
. . . .
    . . . .

«Ладно. Трогай, что ты стал?..»

And then, already moving off,
I saw—Somin took a step
Back from the girl. Baturin, stiff,
Machine pistol at the ready,
Not towards her but away,
Hurled the huge bulk of his body.
Without a plan, in a half-circle,
As if hiding behind each other,
Step by step—two, three, four—
In silence, ever wider, farther.
What's happening? Stooped to collect
      Her things, she turned
      —To understand!
She screamed, down in the snow she fell,
She froze up, curled in a ball,
Like a little animal,
Lying motionless and pale . . .
The firearms had not yet cracked.
An instant passed. Another instant.
I! Why had I waved my hand?
                My God!
           "Driver! Stop!
        Hey there, lads! . . ."
              The automatics.
A burst of fire. Back to their trucks.
 . .   .   .

"Get moving! Why did you pull up?"

Как свежа!.. И в чьем-то доме
Будут ждать ее и след
Вдоль дорог искать. Но Сомин,
Дома не быв много лет,
Тоже ждал и тоже шел,
И к гробам родных пришел.
Как-то немца пожилого
В лес завез он и убил.
И тогда б – довольно слова!..
И тогда я рядом был...
В самом пекле, в самой гуще
Кто же знает – чья вина?..
А откуда? Разве лучше
Из веков она видна?
Кто здесь был – потом рычи,
Кулаком о гроб стучи,
Разрисуют ловкачи –
Нет кому держать за хвост их –
Журналисты, окна РОСТА,
Жданов с платным аппаратом,
Шагинян, Сурков, Горбатов,
Старший фокусник Илья...
Мог таким бы стать и я...
Победим – отлакируют,
Колупай зарытый грех...

So fresh! . . . And soon in someone's house
They'll wait. And then they'll try to trace
Her track along the roads. But he,
Somin, away for years, searched too
And found the graves of his family.
Once he took an old German to a wood
And shot him down there in cold blood.
One word would have prevented that! . . .
I was nearby . . . but in the heat
Of battles, in the thick of hell,
Who knows who's guilty? Who can tell?
But from what distance can one judge? Is
It easier after centuries?
If you're here—well then, snarl later,
Beat your fists upon a grave.
—The cheats will make it all seem better.
We know the way that they'll behave!
Journalists. The ROSTA* posters.
Zhdanov. His paid *apparát*.
Shaginyan, Surkov, Gorbatov,
Ilya,† senior ham of the lot . . .
It might have been me . . . If we win
They'll neatly varnish the whole tale,
Bring to light the hidden sin . . .

*ROSTA (Rossiiskoye Telegrafnoye Agentstvo) : Russian Telegraph Agency,
noted for propaganda posters from early days.

†Andrei Zhdanov, 1896–1949, Secretary of the Central Committee in charge
of propaganda and culture. Marietta Shaginyán, Alexei Surkóv,
Boris Gorbátov: conformist writers. Ilyá: Ilya Ehrenburg.

Все довольны, все пируют –
Что мне надо больше всех?
Всё изгрыз в моем рассудке
Вечный червь – самоанализ...
Может, считанные сутки
В этой жизни мне остались?
Холод чина, суд да власть, –
Как учил индус Чарваки –
А мои плоды и злаки?
А моя когда же часть?
Был «жемчужиной в уборе
Атеистов» тот индус,
И скрестить с ним речи в споре
Я сегодня не найдусь.
Carpe diem! – гедонисты
Нас учили – ДЕНЬ ЛОВИ!
Дни осыпятся, как листья,
Загустеет ток крови.
Все слабей, бледней и реже
Острота и вспышки чувств...
Все так делают. Не мне же
Возражать тебе, индус!
ВСЕ ТАК ДЕЛАЮТ! Бесплодна
Белизна идей и риз:
Жизнь подносит кубок – до дна!
И – сухим раструбом вниз.

When we are satisfied, fed and wined,
Why do I need more than all
Those others the worm that never dies,
The worm of self-analysis,
To chew, torment, destroy my mind?
Perhaps just days, a day, an hour
Remains to me of mortal life . . .
In the chill of rank and power . . .
What was it that Charvaki* taught?
What of my harvest? What of my fruit?
My turn will be upon me, when?
That Indian— "The pearl in the crown
Of Atheists"—I hardly want
To engage him in an argument.
Carpe diem! The hedonists, they
Always taught us—*Seize the day!*
But the days like leaves are falling,
The current of the blood runs thicker.
The sharpness and the strength of feeling
Are growing rarer, paler, weaker . . .
Everyone behaves like that.
Indian, your views I can't refute!
Everyone behaves like that!
To hell with useless purities
—Pure ideas, pure chasubles!
Life offers a drink, so bottoms up!
—Turn down the dry mouth of the cup.

*Legendary founder of the ethical "Charvaka" sect.

Слышишь, слышишь зов упорный,
Шелком скованный, покорный,
Шелестящий, сокровенный:
    «Этот веер черный!
    Веер драгоценный!»
Словно волосы Медузы,
Голова войны лохмата.
Сердце пьяного солдата
Из Советского Союза —
Жальте, жальте, жажды змеи! —
Распахнулся черный веер,
Черный веер Сарасатэ!
В краткий счет секунд и терций
Он нам зноем жизни веет:
    «Ну, какое сердце
    Устоять сумеет?..»

Отобедав, на диване
Затянулся сигаретой,
И в разымчивом тумане
Округляются предметы:
Зеркало и радиола,
В темных изразцах камин.
Белый над кроватью полог.
Пена голубых перин.
Что́ там было... Что́ там будет..
Нет ни завтра, ни вчера.
Пропируем и прокутим

And an insistent call goes on,
Fettered in silk, submissive, fine,
Rustling, deep-concealed within:
      "Here's a fan, a black one!
        It's a very precious fan!"
Yes, like the tresses of Medusa,
Shaggy is the head of War,
To sting the heart of a drunk soldier
Serving the U.S.S.R.:
Sting then, sting, desires like snakes!
Open again the black fan flicks,
The Sarasate fan! Its short
Counting of cadence wafts the heat
Of life towards us, till it close:
      "And, oh, what heart
        Could well oppose? . . ."

On a sofa, after dinner,
I'm puffing at a cigarette.
Patches of smoke float in the air,
Objects all seem rounded out:
The mirror and the radio gleam,
Reflected in the hearth's dark tiles,
And the eiderdown's blue foam,
Where the curtain's whiteness curls.
Who's been here? Who'll be here next? . . .
Yesterday, tomorrow—don't exist.
We'll just feast on and enjoy,

И проспим здесь до утра.
Снежный свет в двойные стекла.
Зимний день уже на склоне.
Как в обернутом бинокле,
Где-то очень далеко,
Старшина в докладном тоне
Хитрым вятским говорком
Рапортует, что расставил
Батарею на постой,
Что жалеючи оставил
Пять семеек за стеной,
Но что тотчас выгнать можно...
Почему-то вдруг тревожно
Сердце вскинулось мое.
Вида не подав наружно,
Спрашиваю равнодушно:
— Женщины?
            — Одно бабьё.
— Молодые?
          С полувзгляда,
Хоть вопрос мой необычен,
Доверительно:
             — Что надо.
Ну, не знаю, как с обличьем.
Вот за то, что ты толков,
И люблю тебя, Хмельков!
Чуть мигни — готовый план:
«Я, товарищ капитан...»

And then sleep till break of day.
Snowy light through double glazing:
The winter day's already passing.
Through the wrong end of a telescope,
From far away I seem to grope
For a beg-to-report voice in the sergeant
Major's cunning Viatka accent,
Telling how he's sorted out
The battery into its billet,
How he's had pity, after all
—Five families—left them inside the wall,
But can evict them any minute . . .
Suddenly, I can't tell why,
My heart is leaping anxiously.
But, giving no external sign,
I ask him quite indifferently,
"Women?"
              "Females, every one."
"Young?"
              He gives me just a glance,
Although the question's—not routine.
He reassures me, "Sure, just fine.
—Well, I haven't had a chance
To check up on their looks, I mean."
Ah, Sergeant Major! Dear Khmelkov,
Your perspicacity I love!
In a twinkling he'd a plan:
"Comrade Captain," he began.

Сформулировать мне трудно;
Так бы смолк и взял бы книгу.
«..Полагаю — в доме людно.
Во дворе видали флигель?
И коровы в хлеве рядом.
Две минуты — и порядок:
Приведу туда любую
Н..надоить нам молока,
Лишь бы, глянувши — какую,
Вы кивнули мне слегка».
Кончено. Не быть покою.
Ласточкою стукоток:
Знать об этом будем двое,
Больше никогда никто.
«Ладно!» — Встал. — «Пошли, Васёк.
Быстро, где они, веди.»
Вышли. Круг. И на порог.
«Ты — поймешь, кого. Следи.»
Пар и брызги пены мыльной.
Утюги. Угар гладильный.
Две кровати. Стол. Корыто.
Боже, сколько их набито!
Не пройти, чтоб не задеть их —
Бабки, мамки, няньки, дети —
Разномастны, разноростны,
От младенцев до подростков, —
Все с дороги сторонятся,

I find formulating hard.
If I said nothing, merely took
Up again that half-read book . . .
"The house is crammed . . . It seems to me:
You see the wing beyond the yard?
The cows are close by in that shed.
Give me two minutes and I'll see
To taking one of them across
To—get milk for us from the cows . . .
First, just come and look them over.
The one you fancy—nod your head."
All's decided. Action, then!
Ah, a fluttering like a swallow:
No one will know, we two alone.
No one else will ever know.
"Right!" I got up. "Let's go, Vasek.
Where are they? —Well, take me quick!"
We went out. Around. And to the door:
"You'll see which one . . . Watch with care!"
Steam and soap and splashing lather.
Irons. The hot fumes steaming off
The ironing. Two beds. Table. Trough.
Good God, how many of them cramped in!
Yes, you can't move without trampling
All the old women, mothers, nurses,
Kids of all colors, ages, sizes,
From babes in arms to adolescents.
Out of my way they all are pressing,

Те не смотрят, те косятся,
Те не сводят глаз с лица
Иноземца-пришлеца.
Стихли крики, речь и гомон,
Лишь шинель моя шуршит.
А Хмельков — как будто дома —
Отвалясь непринужденно,
У двери стоит-следит.
Как неловок! Как смешон я!
Лица женщин обвожу,
Но... т а к о й не нахожу:
Кто сбежал в мороз да в лес,
Кто упрятался вблизи...
И зачем сюда я влез?
Чёрт с ним.. – Э... wie heißen Sie?
Худощавая блондинка,
Жгут белья крутя над ванной,
Чуть оправила косынку
И сказала робко: «Anne».
Так.. лицо.. фигура... Да...
Н е звезда киноэкрана,
            Не звезда...
Лет неплохо бы отбавить,
Здесь и здесь чуток прибавить..
Нос немножко великонек,
Да-к и я ж не Erlkönig.
Шут с ним, ладно, лучше, хуже,
Только б выбраться наружу.
Неразборно что-то буркнув,

Some look away, some look at me
Out of the corner of their eyes,
Others stare quite openly
At this foreigner who's come.
The cries die down, and the talk and bustle,
Only the skirts of my greatcoat rustle,
And Khmelkov, lounging, quite at home,
Watches relaxed from by the door.
How embarrassing! I've become
Quite ridiculous! I look.
But the right one isn't there:
She's fled into the frost, the forest,
Or is hiding somewhere near . . .
—Why did I get involved in this?
The devil take them! "Wie heissen Sie?"
A thinnish blonde is twisting a plait
Of linen over the bath, and she
Turns, shifts the kerchief around her hair,
And she shyly answers, "Anne."
Well, yes . . . face . . . figure . . . all that . . .
Not a star of the silver screen,
          Not a star . . .
She could do with a few years less,
With some more flesh on her here and there,
She has rather too large a nose.
But I'm no Erlkönig, let's be fair!
Oh, it could be worse or better.
The devil take it! Well, I'll be off.

Быстро вышел. Следом юркнул
Старшина. В сенях интимно:
«Всё понятно. Вы – во флигель?»
«Я.. туда, но только ты мне...
Неудобно же... не мигом..»
«Разбираюсь! Я – политик!
Всё в порядочке, идите!»

Нежилое. Флигель выстыл.
Хламно. Сумрачно. Нечисто.
В сундуках разворошёно.
По полам напорошёно.
Острый запах нафталина.
На бок швейная машина.
В верхнем ящике комодном
Перерытое бельё...
До черемухи ль? – походно
Как устроить мне ее?
Поискал. В пыли нашлась
Подушонка на полу.
Койка жесткая. Матрас,
Кем-то брошенный в углу.
Подошел, брезгливо поднял,
Перенес его на койку:
Жизнь подносит кубок – до дна!
И не спрашивай, за сколько...
Снега нарост раздышал я

I went, growling out some vague mutter.
Behind scuttled Sergeant Major Khmelkov,
And in the hall, like a conspirator:
"Quite clear! You'll be in the other wing?"
"I am on my way there . . . But don't . . . The mission
Is a bit awkward . . . Can't hurry the thing."
"I'll see to it! I'm a politician!
Ah yes, everything now is quite
In order—you can get on with it!"

Not lived in. This wing has gone cold.
It's full of rubbish. Dirty. Dim.
They've rifled the trunks, simply hurled
The contents pell-mell around the room.
Sharp scent of mothballs hangs in the air.
A sewing machine lies on its side.
Out of the top of a chest of drawers
Ends of crumpled linen protrude . . .
—And cherry blossom? We're in a war—
I have to arrange things for her fast.
I look around and I find on the floor
A grubby pillow that lies in the dust.
A hard iron bedstead. A mattress spread
Out in the corner. I pick it up,
And carry it, queasily, to the bed.
Bottoms up! Life offers a cup.
But don't ask the price . . . I go and breathe
On the accumulated snow

На стекле до тонкой льдинки,
Вижу: в этой же косынке,
Лишь окутав плечи шалью,
С оцинкованным ведром
Как-то трогательно-тихо
Анна движется двором;
В двух шагах за нею, лихо,
Как присяге верный воин
Старшина идет конвоем.
Глянул пару раз назад –
Чуть из дому невдогляд:
«Не туда! Э! Слышишь, фрау!
Не туда! Шагай направо!»
С тем же самым в кротком взгляде
Выражением печали
Оглянулась – поняла ли,
И прошла к моей засаде.
Дверь раскрыла – на пороге
Я. И удивленно дрогнул
Рот ее. Не то ошибкой
Показалось ей, что здесь я, –
Извиняющей улыбкой
Ей смягчить хотелось, если
Я подумал, что она
Заподозрела меня.
Стали так. Не опуская,
Всё ведро она держала...

On the window till it's a wreath
Of filmy ice.
        So I see how
With the kerchief still around her hair,
With a shawl wrapped around her throat,
Carrying a galvanized pail,
And somehow touchingly quiet,
Anne is moving across the yard.
Boldly, two steps behind her there,
Like a warrior keeping his vow,
The sergeant major marches as guard.
He looks back twice at the other wing,
And when he's nicely out of sight,
"Not that way! Do you hear me, Frau?
Not that way! . . . Step to the right!"
In her meek glance was the same
Expression of a gentle anguish.
She turned. Perhaps understood. She came
—Made her way into my ambush.
She opened the door, and there I was.
—Her lips trembled in surprise.
Did she think it was some error?
With an apologetic smile
She tried to make things easier,
In case I somehow thought that she
Wrongfully suspected me . . .
She went on holding the zinc pail.

В белых клетках шерстяная
Шаль с плеча ее сползала.
Дар и связь немецкой речи
Потупленно потеряв,
Шаль зачем-то приподняв,
Я набросил ей на плечи.
С рук, от стирки не остывших,
Легкий вздымливал парок.
Нерешительно спросивши,
Отступила на порог . . .
Шаг к двери непритворенной,
Затворил ее хлопком,
К действиям приговоренный,
Поманил, не глядя: «Komm!»
Ни пыланья, ни литого
Звона радостного в мышцах . . .
– Стал спиной к постели нищих
И услышал, что – готова . . .

С бледно-синими глазами
Непривычно близко сблизясь,
Я ей поздними словами
Сам сказал: – «Какая низость!»
В изголовье лбом запавши,

From her shoulders slipped the shawl,
Woven of some white-checked wool.
In my confusion I was stuck,
Losing the flow of German speech.
Somehow I could only reach
The shawl, and throw it around her neck.
From her hands, still warm after the wash,
A faintest wisp of steam uncurled.
Questioning, and unsure,
She stepped back toward the threshold . . .
I strode to the still-open door,
And I shut it with a crash.
Condemned to action, without looking,
I just gestured to her, "Komm!"
It wasn't passion, or the firm
Pleasure in the muscles ringing . . .
With my back to the mean bed I
Shortly heard that she—was ready . . .

And after, unnaturally close
To the pale blue of her eyes,
I said to her—too late—"How base!"
Annie, that moment, with her face
Sunk in the pillow, in an unsteady

Анна голосом упавшим
Попросила в этот миг:
«Doch erschießen Sie mich nicht!»

Ах, не бойся, есть уж... а-а-а...
На моей душе душа...

1950

Voice that she could not control,
Begged, "Doch erschiessen Sie mich nicht!"*

Have no fear . . . For— Oh!— already
Another's soul is on my soul . . .

1950

---

*Just don't shoot me!

Translator's Note

Prussian Nights was written, or rather composed, in Solzhenitsyn's head, while he was serving his sentence of forced labor. A poem, a verse narrative, it is not autobiography in any strict sense, but it is based on his own war experience. Solzhenitsyn's battery formed part of the Second Byelorussian Front, which invaded East Prussia from the south in January 1945. The attack reached Neidenburg (now Nidzica) on January 20, Allenstein (now Olsztyn) on January 22, and the Baltic—cutting off the German armies in East Prussia—on January 26. Solzhenitsyn was arrested in this area in early February, three weeks after the beginning of the offensive.

There is much in *Prussian Nights* that may be strange to the Western reader, but little that will be obscure. In fact, the only important matter which seems to require explanation is Solzhenitsyn's repeated use of the nineteenth-century Spanish violinist and composer Sarasate. Solzhenitsyn takes an air of his, running naturally through his own mind, as the persistent voice of conscienceless temptation, accompanying the wartime urges to self-indulgent destructiveness and sensuality.

The only other reference which may be obscure is Solzhenitsyn's appeal to Charvaki, eponymous founder of the Charvaka sect, without a god, but with a devotion to ethical principle and personal responsibility. They, too, are far less known in the West than among the Russian intelligentsia. To them Solzhenitsyn turns for just such principles, to which he had and has so powerful an affinity, as against the pressures and temptations which then surrounded him.

* * *

The difficulties of verse translation are notorious. As W. H. Auden pointed out of Cavafy, the central problem is to get the tone. But this interlocks with the technical difficulties. Ideally, we must also preserve literalness, and rhyme and tempo.

These requirements tend to conflict, to put it mildly. Even though literalness is a more slippery conception than might appear (allowing, for example, for the different connotations of similar words and the equivalence of different similes in different languages), I have departed minimally from Solzhenitsyn's text.

But there could be no question whatever of making an unrhymed translation, or one which did not preserve the meter. The whole movement of the verse made rhyme and meter quite essential—and it is a type of versification, in any case, which is common to English and other languages, and even central to a certain international tradition.

The main column of the poem is in ballad meter, usually with alternating masculine and feminine rhymes; but there are frequent variations of structure. The meter, and the tempo, particularly in the sections dealing with the soldiery and their advance into East Prussia, are of a breathless, reckless sort. At the other end of the long front, I chanced to see the Russian columns pushing ahead in the Balkans, and nothing could be more appropriate in catching the devil-may-care spirit which marked them. The meter (as against the rhyme scheme) only alters once, formally marking the tragedy of the Russian ex-prisoners of war as they are marched back to the labor camps. But, though the meter does not otherwise change, the feeling and tempo do, in a way which I hope I have managed to render.

Russian is a language a good deal richer in rhyme than English. To compensate for this, the normal four-line English ballad meter traditionally requires a rhyme only every second line, as we see both in popular anonymity, from "Sir Patrick Spens" to "Frankie and Johnnie" and "St. James Infirmary Blues," and in the work of conscious poets from Coleridge's "The Rime of the Ancient Mariner" to the ballads of Auden and Yeats. Where this regular form is maintained, I have usually had to be content with that, while seeking to fill out the other two where I could do so without distorting the tone or meaning. Where, as is frequent, the four-line form is departed from—in couplets, five-line "verses," and so on—I have sought a higher proportion of rhyme. More generally, the problem in each has been to find the rhymes necessary to keep the poem moving at the correct swing, without any but the rarest, smallest, and most unavoidable deviations from the meaning, or contortions of the movement.

The principles of rhyme in Russian are the same as in English. The departure from pure rhyme which has marked both languages in the past couple of generations takes different forms. It is usual in recent Russian poetry to treat as rhyme, or the equivalent of rhyme, a retention of rhyme on the stressed syllable with any amount of variation on the unstressed, as in such doublets or triplets as "spiral" and "tyro," "madam" and "had its," "tavern," "savage," and "have its."

A reasonably typical example from *Prussian Nights* may
be seen in the lines

> Bez razvedki i bez khleba
> Gnali v nogi Lyudendorfu,
> A potom pod sinim nebom
> Ikh toplili v chernom torfe.

> Without reconnaissance and without bread
> They drove [them] under the feet of Ludendorff,
> And then under a blue sky
> They drowned them in the black peat.

But we also find further departures: "zharit" and "sharyat";
"strakhe" and "sakhar"; "mekhom" and "potekhu";
"zaklyustan" and "pustit"; "Baturin," "figuroy," and
"Amure"; "sblizas' " and "nizost'."

To the English ear these would not be acceptable. Our own
extension of permissible rhyme has been in the direction of
accepting weak rhymes ("is," "centuries"; "christened,"
"homeland"), and assonance, as in Yeats's "stone" and
"man," "days" and "these," or (in eight successive lines of
a single ballad, the other four being unrhymed) "stood,"
"dead," "swore," "poor." In this I have naturally followed the
English rather than the Russian usage.

There is one special difficulty for any translator into
English—he is translating into a language in which usages on
the two sides of the Atlantic are not always the same. I have as
far as possible tried to avoid wording which is not readily

understandable to both Britons and Americans. But sometimes it has been impossible to avoid this: for example, in military terminology I have used the British "brigade" and "troop."

These are no more than some technical notes on the translation, showing that, always firmly within the major problem of dealing with the whole, each line presents its own problem, to be more or less satisfactorily resolved. Imperfect as any rendering must be, this one may yet, I hope, give a true and fair echo of the original. But it need hardly be said that perfection is unattainable, that the original is superior, and that any defects readers find in this remarkable poem should be attributed to the translator and not to the author.

Thanks on the matter of the translation are due above all to Dr. Elisabeth Robson, who thoroughly worked the Russian text over for me, and without whose profound and subtle knowledge of the language this version could never have been produced; to Mr. Michael Scammell for much valuable comment and criticism; to Mr. Max Hayward, Miss Patricia Blake, Dr. Frederick Starr, Mrs. Edythe Holbrook, Mr. Kingsley Amis, Miss Carolyn Kizer, Mr. Alexis Klimoff, and Miss Nancy Meiselas, who read the translation in draft and made a number of useful suggestions; and finally to Alexander Solzhenitsyn himself, whose comments were naturally the most fruitful of all.